by Maria Leach

drawings by Kurt Werth

THE
LUCK
BOOK

A YEARLING BOOK

A YEARLING BOOK

Published by
Dell Publishing Co., Inc.
1 Dag Hammarskjold Plaza
New York, New York 10017

Yearling ® TM 913705, Dell Publishing Co., Inc.

ISBN: 0-440-45103-5

Reprinted by arrangement with William Collins + World
Publishing Co., Inc., (a subsidiary of William Collins
Limited).

Printed in the United States of America

First Yearling printing—April 1979

CW

CONTENTS

What Is Luck?   7
CHANGING LUCK   16
SCHOOL LUCK   20
JUST HIS LUCK   24
STREET LUCK   25
THE LUCKY BEGGAR   33
LOVE LUCK   34
BAD LUCK PUT INTO THE BAG   39
BIRTHDAY LUCK   44
FRIDAY   47
WHICH?   51
HOLIDAY LUCK   52
FOOL'S LUCK   58
JEAN SOT   60
POOR OLD CRICKET!   63
THE LUCKY MAN   66
MONEY LUCK   70
MAKING YOUR OWN   73
LUCKIER AND LUCKIER   75
NOTHING TO LOSE   81
EVERYDAY LUCK   84

THE LUCKY SHIRT   92
MAKE A WISH   94
BE CAREFUL!   100
THIRTEEN   102
Author's Notes and Bibliography   109

WHAT IS LUCK?

> For all that I can tell, said he,
> Is that it is a mystery . . .

The concept of luck must be about as old as the mind of man. But all through the centuries no one has been able to say what luck *is*. It is the one element in human life that defies all explanation.

Luck is a marvel and a mystery. Luck is that strange and unseen power that piles up the good things of life for one man and leaves the next man miserable and deprived. One man has good luck, regardless of worth or effort; and another, just as good a man or better, has bad luck. Who can explain this? Who can explain it away? The marvel and the mystery and the fact remain.

But the very reality of luck and the haphazard way things happen, or *happen to happen*, have led people through the ages to personify luck and set up a god or goddess of luck who could be prayed to, or who might be pleased in some way, enticed to favor oneself, by little formulistic rigmaroles or acts.

The Romans had Fortuna, goddess of luck. They pictured her holding a cornucopia in one hand and from it strewing luck with the other. Sometimes she was shown blindfolded to symbolize the unreason of her giving. The Greeks thought of their god Hermes as a bringer of quick riches.

Lakshmi is the name of the Hindu goddess of luck, still worshiped in some parts of India today. She is the giver of fortune and good luck; but sometimes (for what unknown reason) she bestows bad luck as well. Because she is beautiful, she is usually pictured with two arms; but as Lakshmi, the bounteous giver, she is sometimes shown with four.

In Japan there are seven gods of luck. There is Benten, the only woman among them, who brings beauty to girls and women; Ebisu fishes up the fish of good luck out of the sea; Bishamon and Daikoku bring wealth; Fuku-roku-ju and Jurojin give health and long life. But fat little bald-headed Hotei with his bag of treasures is the favorite god of luck. Sometimes the bag is full of gold; sometimes it is full of children! He gives wonderful things to people who do not worry. You can buy him in many shops: little carved wooden images of Hotei with his grin and his fat little belly. You are supposed to rub his belly for good luck. It gets very shiny.

The Tlingit Indians on the North Pacific Coast of North America used to pray to the grampus for good luck in hunting seals.

We may not believe in gods of luck today, but we do believe in luck. All through the ages people have thought: *How can you get what you want? What can one do to make certain things come to pass?* How do you bring good luck and prevent bad? How do you find love and keep it? How do you make wishes come true in real life—not just in dreams? (Even the pig dreams of acorns, the Irish say.) And the old Micmac Indians of the Maritimes used to believe that there is one moment, one special moment, in everyone's life, when the uttered wish comes true.

And so there exist thousands and thousands and thousands of special magic ways, little charms and spells and formulas and gestures, by which we hope, and often enough *expect*, to get luck on our side and make things turn out happily and right. You know all about the many luck objects that people carry and pretend not to rely on: the rabbit's foot, the four-leaf clover, lucky pennies, horseshoes, lucky rings, a baby's shoe dangling in the windshield, a buckeye (horse chestnut) in the pocket. We try everything three times—the third time for luck. "The third time never fails." We knock on wood to take the bad luck off a brag. Drop a glove, meet your love. And, of course, always cross your fingers while lying.

This book could not possibly cover, or even mention, all the world's store of luck lore. Just in Germany alone more than a thousand proverbs and folk sayings about luck have been collected.

All the many sayings and beliefs about what is good luck or bad luck for a baby, for instance, have had to be passed over. But always carry the baby upstairs once before he is taken down, they say, so that he will rise in the world. Lucky and unlucky colors have been passed over also, but here is a sample:

> Marry in red, you'll wish you were dead
> Marry in white, you are doing all right
> Marry in green, ashamed to be seen
> Marry in yellow, ashamed of the fellow
> Marry in blue, always be true.

Blue is true love's color, evidently, for in South Carolina they used to say: if her eyes are blue, she'll always be true.

How to be lucky at card games is also omitted. But everyone knows that to get up and walk around your chair changes your luck at cards.

Wedding and marriage signs and sayings, and dos and don'ts for good luck, are too numerous to include. But everyone says, "Happy is the bride that the sun shines on." Very widespread is the belief that to ensure a happy future every bride should wear

Something old, something new
Something borrowed and something blue.

But it is bad luck to try on your sister's wedding dress; if you do, you will never be married yourself.

Even the categories of daily life in which luck functions are too many to list. There are all kinds of luck charms and spells associated with birth and death and funerals. There is a huge mass of luck lore connected with making and wearing clothes and hats and shoes, with washing dishes, dropping dishcloths, breaking and looking into mirrors, sweeping, farming, fishing, building fires. If a girl knows how to start a clean quick fire, she will get a good husband quick! Did you ever notice that the smoke from a yard bonfire follows the child who lies or breaks a promise? This is only one of the many reasons why it is bad luck to lie or break a promise.

Spit and spitting are very important in warding off evil and making good-luck charms and spells work for sure. Spit on your fishhook to make the fish bite. Fighters everywhere, from the ancient Roman arena to Madison Square Garden, spit on their hands for luck before going into a fight. Most schoolboys do this too. Can you spit straight up in the air? This is a sure way to prevent broken promises—given or received. Then there are all the dos and taboos for luck connected with animals and birds and insects and with plants. Peoples in every part of the world have these and no one book could tell them all.

It is bad luck to kill a robin or a wren or a swallow or to harm one or to harm their nests. An English proverb says:

> He that hurts robin, swallow, or wren,
> Will never prosper, boy or man.

It is bad luck to kill a cat. And it is generally thought to be bad luck for a black cat to cross your path. But it is lucky to own a black cat and very lucky to sleep with one, although some people think this is bad.

If you see a beetle on his back, waving his legs, it is good luck to turn him over and let him go on his way. You are lucky if a butterfly lights on you. And of course, never, never kill a spider.

> If you want to live and thrive,
> Let the spider run alive.

If one lights on you, she brings you money.

If a black-and-white dog crosses your path on your way to some business, that means the business will have success. If a strange dog follows you home, it is a sign of wealth on its way. Take him in and be good to him to make sure that omen comes true. The old Kwakiutl Indians say that to hit a dog causes swollen wrists.

Everybody knows that the four-leaf clover is lucky: lucky to find, lucky to keep, bad luck to give away. Many people say wear it in your shoe for luck—preferably the left shoe. Don't smell a tiger lily unless you want freckles. It is bad luck to interfere with or break into a fairy ring. You know what a fairy ring is: that pretty dark green circle on a lawn or in a field where fairies have danced at night. It is caused by a certain fungus and is usually surrounded by a ring of mushrooms. Catch a falling leaf and keep it. You will be happy as long as you keep it. The best way to raise turnips is to take hold of the tops and pull.

There are magic charms and formulas everywhere in the world designed to cure illness, get rid of enemies, bring you love or money or gifts or letters, to protect you from harm, to win games, pass exams, and to make wishes come true. And however much today we deny or are shamefaced about these many beliefs and acts, still most people behave as if there were some deep truth in them. Doesn't everybody wish on his own birthday candles?

Never pass by your first luck.

JAMAICA NEGRO

When Fortune comes, open the doors.

The doctor can cure disease, but not bad luck.

CHINA

Anything begrudged is never lucky.

IRELAND

*Luck is a cow: Front end to some,
     hind end to others.*

ITALY

*If you haven't got good judgment,
     you're lucky to have good legs.*

ITALY

A windy March is lucky . . . Let it blow!

SOUTH CAROLINA NEGRO

Pluck makes luck.

A bold heart ever did fetch luck halfway.

GULLAH NEGRO

Diligence is the mother of good luck.

Your luck is in yourself.

Luck say: Open your mouth and shut your eyes.

GEORGIA NEGRO

Give a man luck and throw him in the sea.

ENGLAND

15

CHANGING LUCK

1.

Once there was a traveler going about in the world, who one day entered a town and saw a great crowd gathered around the door of a little church.

He wondered what was going on, so he, too, joined the crowd.

He saw a tall young girl dressed as a bride, with a fancy tall comb in her hair to hold the veil. She was sitting on the church steps weeping as if she could never stop. The young bridegroom was standing by, looking pretty glum and doing nothing. The people in the crowd were murmuring to each other and shaking their heads and saying "tch, tch."

"What is the matter here?" said the young man.

"Oh, my terrible misfortune!" sobbed the girl. "I shall die an old maid!"

And she stood up to show the stranger just what the matter was.

"I am too tall!" she said. "And the beautiful high comb will not go through the door!" And she fell to sobbing again.

So the young fellow grabbed the comb out of her hair, threw the veil any which way over her head,

gave her a slap—so she ducked her head—and a shove—so she shot through the door. The young bridegroom leaped in after her, and the bystanders, amazed, walked in after them.

No doubt the young couple were married in there, and got out again somehow, and lived happily ever after.

That young fellow certainly changed that girl's luck for her. Perhaps there is always something one can do about it.

2.

Once there was a young fellow going along a road. It was evening and nearly dark, and he saw a farmhouse nearby with a light in the window. So he went in and asked if he could get some supper.

An old couple and a girl were just about to sit down to a good supper of hot biscuits, tea, and jam, so they said, "Sure. You're welcome." Could he spend the night? "Sure. You're welcome."

So they sat down to supper, and although the old people were polite they seemed worried. Every once in a while they would glance up into the rafters.

The young fellow glanced up, too, but all he saw was a good stout ax hanging in the rafters.

"That's our bad luck up there," they told him, when they saw him look up.

"Day after day, year in and year out, we sit under that ax, and someday it might fall and kill us," said the old woman.

"It is terrible bad luck to live our lives under the ax," said the old man. "Who knows what minute it may fall and kill one of us?"

Just then the young girl burst into tears. "And suppose I should marry you and have a child! It could fall and kill the baby!"

The old woman started to cry, too, and the old man sighed.

"Bad luck hangs over our heads," he said.

So the young fellow stood up in the little low room, and he reached up and took the ax down out of the rafters.

"There!" he said.

The old people were overjoyed, and the young girl wanted him to stay and get married. But the young fellow just walked to the door.

"All right," he said. "I'll come back and marry you, when I find three people as silly as you."

The young fellow did meet up with silly people in his travels, but that makes a long story. This is enough to show that when bad luck hangs over your head the only way out is to do something about it.

SCHOOL LUCK

Schoolchildren all over the United States and Canada, in Europe and the British Isles, and in many other places in the world have thought up a lot of secret ways to change their luck.

Here are a few of the things they recommend:

1. Wear your sweater backward, or wrong side out, for good luck in exams.

2. Lace your sneakers from the top down to help you pass your exams. This helps you win the game, too, if you happen to be on one of the school athletic teams.

3. Wear the same hat, tie, sweater, socks, sneakers, or shoes—or the same something—to every game of the season. This is a good-luck charm to help your school win.

4. In South Carolina they say that if you drop a book on the way to school, that is a sign that you will do your lessons wrong.

5. In England, some children say if you see a spotted dog on the way to school cross your fingers and you will pass the exams.

6. Almost everywhere children say if you sleep with your book under your pillow you will remember what is in it in the morning and surely pass *that* exam.

The Pennsylvania Dutch say: never leave your book lying open when you go to bed, or everything you have learned from it will run out.

7. To pass your exams, wear the same dress you wore when you passed before, or use the same pencil you used when you passed before. Some children have an old "lucky pencil" worn down to a stub which they save just to use for exams.

8. And some children use a brand-new pencil for exams, because a new one has never written anything wrong; it has never made a mistake.

9. Sit in the same seat you sat in when you passed before, and you will pass again.

10. Change your shoe from left to right; that is, on exam day, wear the left shoe on the right foot and the right shoe on the left foot. There was a great fad for this in Plainfield, New Jersey, one year recently. Everybody did it.

11. One teen-ager in Barrington, Nova Scotia, told me, "I always take a rose to school on exam day

for luck." This, of course, would be for some final exam in June.

12. Another teen-ager from Schenectady, New York, told me that once she wore her smart brother's tie pin to school for luck in her hardest exam. It worked.

13. In North Carolina they say you will be lucky in exams if you wear socks that don't match on exam day: one white and one blue one, for instance, or one red and one brown.

14. Once I asked a little girl eleven years old what she did for luck in exams. And she said, "Study."

JUST HIS LUCK

One night a weary traveler was overtaken by dark. He was so tired that he could walk no farther to look for an inn. So he lay down by the side of the road and went to sleep.

He did not notice that he had lain down at the edge of a deep well.

But his Luck (the luck good or bad that follows every man) saw that he was about to turn over in his sleep and roll into the well. So Luck woke him.

"Wake up!" said Luck. "Wake up."

The man woke up and wondered who had called him. He reached out his hand in the dark and felt the edge of the well.

"Just my luck if I had fallen into it!" he said.

"That's the way it goes," said Luck. "Every man blames bad luck for his own carelessness!"

24

STREET LUCK

1. Never walk backward in the street or on a road.
It's bad luck for your father and mother.

2. Don't step on a crack, either.

> Step on a crack
> Break your mother's back.

This rime is evidently still known and chanted
everywhere in the United States from New England to Texas and from the Atlantic to the Pacific.
During World War I, New York City children
were stepping on cracks as often as possible and
saying:

> Step on a crack
> Break the Kaiser's back.

During World War II they chanted:

> Step on a crack
> Break old Hitler's back.

It seems to have worked in both wars.

3. This latter rime has been reported to the author from Nebraska, too. Probably it was as widespread as the original rime.

4. In Texas they say:

> Step on a crack
> Break your mother's back.
> Step in a hole
> Break the sugar bowl.

5. Children in various parts of the British Isles say it is unlucky to step on a crack for three reasons: 1) you will do your lessons wrong all day, 2) your hair will fall out, 3) you will fall downstairs.

6. Almost all over the world people still say it means bad luck if a black cat crosses your path. Whether you believe this or not, just say, "Black cat, bring me luck." And it will.

7.
> See a pin and pick it up
> All the day you'll have good luck.
> See a pin and let it lay
> You'll have bad luck all the day.

—or, in North Carolina:

Bad luck follows all the day.

Sticklers for grammar have changed the last two lines to:

> See a pin and let it lie
> You'll need a pin before you die.
> > or
> You'll have bad luck until you die.
> > or
> All the day good luck will fly.
> > or
> All the day you'll have to cry.
> > or
> All your luck will pass you by.

8. If you pass by a pin in the street, you are just turning your back on luck. Some people say it is a sign of good luck if the point is toward you, bad luck if it points away.

9. It is bad luck to pick up a handkerchief, if you see one lying in the street. If you pick it up, you will soon need it. Something will happen to make you cry.

10. It is good luck to see a white horse. Just to *see* one means you will receive a gift, or find money, or

get your dearest wish, or something. And to see one is luckier than ever nowadays, when one hardly sees *any* color horse in a street (city, town, or village) at all. So of course it is also truer than ever that if you can count one hundred white horses in a day, you will find money.

It used to be that every child, when he saw a white horse, made a cross on the ground with his toe or a stick, spit in it, then stamped on it(or performed some such formula, ancient, modern, or of his own invention)—and really expected a gift!

11. Nowadays some children say, instead, that it is good luck to see a white car.

12. It is also good luck to see a horse with four white feet. A horse (any color) with four white feet was considered so lucky in the old days that he and his driver and the load were allowed to pass through any toll gate (bridge or highway) without paying the toll fee.

13. It is good luck to see a load of hay approaching. Make a wish and don't look at it again after wishing. Say:

> Load of hay, load of hay
> I make a wish and turn away.

But never tell your wish to anyone or it will not come true.

14. New Jersey children say: make a wish on a load of hay and hold your breath till it passes by. You will not get the wish if you breathe before it passes.

15. In Ireland they say it is good luck to find a white button in the street.

16. In Italy it is good luck to see a *gobbo* (a hunchback)—especially in the evening. Italians have a little rime:

> *Gobbo di sera*
> *Fortuna vera.*
> (Hunchback in the evening
> Good Luck.)

And it brings extra good luck to touch one.

17. Another good-luck charm from Italy is to walk between two *carabinieri* (cops). In Italy policemen walk the streets in pairs, in very fancy, magnificent uniforms. You hardly ever get a chance to walk between them because they walk very close together. But sometimes, when they see a small child,

they separate just to let the youngster run between them for luck.

18. Don't let a post or hydrant or a telephone pole, or even another person, come between you and your companion while walking together. It breaks the friendship, they say. So say "Bread and butter" to each other to keep off the bad luck.

19. It is good luck to find a penny in the street. Pick it up and keep it. That is your luck penny. It is especially good to wear this penny in your shoe. And if it hurts, put it inside your loafer strap.

20. If you have been having a streak of bad luck, or feel one coming on, hammer a nail, or even a pin, into a telephone pole. This may be easier for town or country children to do than for city children, because sometimes in big cities the telephone poles are made of steel. This comforting and convenient custom is reported from San Mateo, California. I wonder if children anywhere else in the United States do it?

THE LUCKY BEGGAR

Once there was a beggar wandering around from one place to another. One night as dark fell, he saw a very nice farmhouse by the side of the road.

He knocked on the door and asked for a place to sleep. But the farmer said, "No!" and slammed the door.

The poor old beggar thought this was awfully bad luck. He turned away, grumbling.

"How unlucky I am," he said, but he found a comfortable place to sleep against a haystack nearby.

That night somehow the farmer's house burned down. He lost all that he had and barely escaped with his life.

"How lucky I am," said the beggar in the morning.

LOVE LUCK

1. Do you crave dill pickles? If you do, you are in love.

2. Does your boy (or girl) friend love you? There are lots of ways of finding out.

One is the old-time game called Cancellation. You can play it by yourself, or you and the one you love can play it together. Here is the way to play it.

Write your full name on a piece of paper, and write your friend's name under it.

Cancel out the like letters in both names (each *a* in yours for each *a* in his, for instance). Then count the remaining letters in each name, saying: *friendship, courtship, marriage, love, hate.* Write down the last word said after each name. These two words reveal the state of affairs between you two.

Here are a few examples to show how it is done and how things turn out.

Mary Williams   *friendship*
John Turner   *love*

Mary is friendly toward John and John loves Mary.

| Florence Brown | *courtship* |
| Richard Grafton | *marriage* |

They're courting and are likely to marry.

| Margaret Robinson | *love* |
| George O'Connell | *courtship* |

George is courting Margaret and she already loves him.

3. Name the bedposts for four boys you like, and the post you see first when you wake up in the morning will be the one you will marry.

4. If your shoelace comes untied, your true love is thinking of you.

5. If you give your boy (or girl) friend a pair of gloves, it is a signal that your love is true love and will last forever.

6. If the one you love happens to sneeze while saying "I love you," it is the truth.

"Sneezing to the truth" is a very ancient belief. In the wonderful story of the *Odyssey*, Penelope's son sneezed at the end of her prayer for the safe return of Odysseus. And Penelope took the sneeze for a sign her prayer would come true—as it did.

7. To dream of roses means that someone (you know who) loves you. This is what they say in Arkansas.

8.   Stub your toe
           Kiss your thumb,
           And your true love
           Will surely come.

9. To dream of a bright, lighted candle means that you will have a letter from your love tomorrow, or very soon.

10. Then of course there is the old-time way of telling whether someone loves you or not by pulling all the petals off a daisy. You say "He (she) loves me, he loves me not" alternately until the last petal

is pulled off. Whatever you say for the last petal tells whether he/she loves you or not.

Sometimes children do not play fair with this method of finding out if they are loved. Sometimes, if the last petal says, "——loves me not," a child will take another daisy, and even then another, till the last petal gives the wished-for answer.

11. To make someone love you:

Take red-rose leaves and white-rose leaves and forget-me-nots. Boil in 365 drops of water (one drop for each day of the year) for 1/16 of an hour (that is, about 3¾ minutes). Put three drops of this in the coffee, tea, milk, Coke, or whatever the person is about to drink. It will make him/her surely love you.

12. Get a lock of your boy (or girl) friend's hair (even one hair will do) and sew it into your dress, or jacket, and he (or she) will be crazy about you.

13. Steal your boy (or girl) friend's shoes and wear them yourself for a little while, but be sure that no one else puts them on before you get a chance to return them—OR ELSE, he/she will love that one instead.

14. When a boy takes a girl for a ride in an automobile, he has a right to kiss her every time they

pass a one-eyed car (a car with only one head-light).

15. Do they still say it is all right for a boy to kiss a girl if she puts on his hat? They do say if she puts on his hat on purpose, she *wants* to be kissed.

16. And, of course, it is all right for the boys to kiss the girls under the mistletoe during the Twelve Days of Christmas: December 25-January 6.

BAD LUCK
PUT INTO THE BAG

Once there were two brothers who, at the proper time, got married and went their ways. As time went by, one became very poor, and one became very rich.

The poor brother had a tired wife, many children, little to eat. Nothing that he undertook turned out well. He grew poorer and poorer.

So one day he went to his rich brother and asked for help.

"No," said the rich brother. "You must make your own way in the world."

Then after a while the poor man came to the rich one again and said, "Lend me a horse for one day, for I have no way to plow my field."

"All right. Take a horse for one day," said the rich brother.

So the poor brother went down to the rich brother's field to find a horse, and there he saw a strong man plowing his brother's field with the horses.

"Who are you?" said the poor man.

"I am your brother's Luck," said the man. "I see to the work and he does not have to bother with it."

"What about my Luck?" said the poor man.

"There is your Luck," said the man, pointing at a skinny little man in a red shirt asleep under a bush.

"I'll fix him!" said the poor man, and he picked up a stick and gave the fellow a whack.

Luck woke up.

"What's the matter?" he said.

"Look at my brother's Luck plowing the field, while you sleep!" said the poor man.

"Well, don't expect me to plow!" said the poor man's Luck. "But I'll help you to trade."

"Trade? I have nothing to trade."

"We'll take your wife's old dress and sell it; with that money we'll buy a new one and sell it. Then we'll buy a better one and sell that—and so on and on. I'll help you."

"All right," said the poor man.

The next day the man and his wife packed up what little they had, washed the children's faces, and started off for town to engage in trade.

As they turned away they heard the sound of weeping.

"Who is that weeping?" said the man.

"I am your bad luck. My name is Misery."

"Why are you weeping?"

"Because you are leaving me behind."

"Well, come along!" said the man. "Hand me that bag, wife. Dump the things out."

The wife dumped her poor possessions on the ground and gave the man the bag.

"Crawl in," said the man. Old Misery crawled into the bedraggled old sack and the man tied up the mouth of it tight with a string.

"There!" he said to his wife. "There's our bad luck in the bag!" And he buried the bag in the earth beside the old hut.

Then off they went to town, the man and his family. And the man began to trade just as he had been told to do. He sold his wife's old dress for a small sum. With that he managed to buy one a little better, which he sold for a little more. And so it went: one lucky deal after another.

And gradually the poor man became a rich man.

In time his brother heard the news and came to town to visit him. And he saw that his once-poor brother was now richer than himself.

"You were poor! Your family was starving!" he cried. "How did you get rich?"

"I put my bad luck in a bag and buried it," said the town brother, laughing.

"Where?"

"Beside the old hut."

The other said good-bye and started home. His heart was filled with envy and jealousy. He could not bear for his brother to be the richer one.

He drove straight to his brother's old hut and

dug up the bag. He untied the tight knot and set bad luck free.

"Go find my brother," he cried. "Go take his wealth. Hurry!"

"Oh, no!" said bad luck. "I'd rather stay with you."

This story has a moral, I suppose, or two morals. One is that no matter how bad your luck is, you can somehow get the best of it. The other is that bad luck turns and follows the grudging envious heart.

BIRTHDAY LUCK

1. Whatever day of the week you were born on, that is *your* lucky day.

2. In Louisiana they say it is good luck to be born on Halloween.

3. In Devonshire, England, about one hundred years ago, it was considered very lucky to be born on Christmas.

4. Here are some birth-omen rimes for the days of the week:

Monday's child is fair of face,
Tuesday's child is full of grace,
Wednesday's child is loving and giving,
Thursday's child must work for a living,
Friday's child is full of woe,
Saturday's child has a journey to go,
But the child who is born on the Sabbath day
Is merry and happy and wise and gay.

5. Friday's child, however, is often said to be loving and giving, although it is widely considered

unlucky, except in Maryland, to be born on a Friday.

6. It is good luck for the child who blows out all the candles on his birthday cake with one breath. He must make a wish, and if all the candles go out with one puff, the wish will come true. But he must not tell the wish.

7. Always put an extra candle in the middle of the birthday cake. If you are eleven years old, for instance, there should be eleven candles around the edge of your cake (one for each year) and one in the middle *to grow on*.

8. A child has to be spanked on his birthday: as many whacks as he is years old, plus one hard one to grow on.

9. It brings you luck if someone gives you white flowers on your birthday.

10. Never cry on your birthday—no matter what. If you do, something will happen to make you cry every day for a year.

11. It is good luck to wear your own birthstone. Here are the birthstones for every month of the year:

January	garnet
February	amethyst
March	bloodstone or aquamarine
April	diamond or sapphire
May	emerald
June	pearl or moonstone
July	ruby
August	sardonyx or chrysolite
September	sapphire
October	opal (It is unlucky to own or wear an opal unless it is your birthstone.)
November	topaz
December	turquoise or lapis lazuli

FRIDAY

Almost everybody everywhere in America and Europe says that Friday is a bad-luck day.

Don't get born on a Friday—if you can help it. Friday's child is either full of sin or full of woe, they say.

Don't get married on a Friday. Nothing will turn out well. "Marry on Friday, marry for losses," says the old rime.

Don't laugh on Friday, they say in Italy.

> Laugh on Friday
> Sigh on Saturday
> Weep on Sunday.

Don't sneeze on Friday. The old rimes say:

> Sneeze on Friday, sneeze for sorrow.

Don't cut your fingernails on Friday, either. Cut them on Friday, cut them for sorrow—or—for woe.

Some say:

Cut them on Friday, cut them for losses.

Others say: . . . for crosses.

In North Carolina, South Carolina, Kentucky, New York, and Nebraska, you cut them for sorrow; in Maryland, Ontario, New England, Pennsylvania, and Iowa, if you cut them on Friday, you cut them for woe.

In Quebec they say for disappointment.

But in Massachusetts, Illinois, Texas, California, and New Mexico, it is just plain bad luck to cut your fingernails on a Friday.

Don't start anything on a Friday. Either you will never finish it or something will go wrong. Friday is a bad day for beginnings, especially journeys—and some say it is especially bad to start on a journey by water on a Friday.

Don't cut out a dress on Friday. If you do, you'll have a disappointment before you wear it.

Don't plant anything on a Friday.

It is bad luck to turn your bed on a Friday. If you do, it won't be comfortable.

What about that child born on a Friday: is he always unlucky? True, the rimes say that Friday's child is full of sin or full of woe, but in one of the traditional English rimes about the days of the week, *Friday's child is loving and giving.* And what could be nicer than that?

Friday must really be a lucky day for the United States.

Christopher Columbus first set sail on his fa-

mous voyage across the Atlantic on Friday, August 3, 1492. On Friday, October 12, 1492, he first caught sight of land in a brand-new world—a little island in the Bahamas which he named San Salvador.

On Friday, January 4, 1493, he set sail on the long trip back across the ocean, and on Friday, March 15, he arrived safely home in Palos, Spain.

Columbus made a second voyage and sighted Hispaniola on Friday, November 22, 1493. A little more than six months later, still lured westward in hopes of finding Asia, on Friday the twelfth of June, 1494, Columbus found the vast land which he knew was no island, but a continent, and which we now know was America.

Seventy-one years later, Pedro Menéndez founded St. Augustine, Florida, the oldest town in the United States, on Friday, September 7, 1565.

Another fifty-five years later, the Pilgrims disembarked from a little sailing vessel called the *Mayflower* and stepped ashore onto Plymouth Rock on Friday, December 22, 1620.

Two more Fridays of importance to the United States were Friday, February 22, 1732, when George Washington was born, and Friday, October 19, 1781, when Cornwallis surrendered to him at Yorktown, Virginia.

WHICH?

Once there was a very rich man. He lived in a big house, dressed with magnificence, and feasted daily. He owned many ships which sailed in and out of all the ports in the world and brought back more and more riches. Everything the man turned to was a success. And his wealth heaped up.

One day his neighbor, a poor man, came to him and said, "Which is better: luck or cleverness?"

"Don't talk to me about luck!" said the rich man. "Don't sit around waiting for luck! Everything I possess I got through my own diligence and cleverness."

That night there was a great storm at sea. All the man's ships sank to the bottom with their rich cargoes. The next day he was cheated in a business deal and lost his fortune. About a week later his house burned down with everything in it. He barely escaped with his life.

Well? Which? Luck or cleverness?

HOLIDAY LUCK

New Year's Day (JANUARY 1)

In nearly all the southern United States, blacks and whites alike are said to eat black-eyed peas and hog jowls on New Year's Day for luck for a year.

In North Carolina it is customary to eat goose on New Year's for luck. Eat goose for New Year's dinner and you will be rich, they say.

In Texas they say never eat chicken on New Year's, because a chicken has to scratch for a living.

In New England sauerkraut and pork used to be eaten to ensure a year's worth of luck and money.

In France on New Year's Day, pancakes were tossed on a griddle and eaten for luck and wealth.

The first foot to enter a house on New Year's Day brings either good or bad luck, and to leave the house before a visitor has come in brings very bad luck indeed.

In Italy it is good luck if the first foot to enter is a man, bad luck if the first visitor is a woman.

In Rome on New Year's Eve, at midnight, the people pitch the old bad luck of the past out the windows in order to start the new year right. All over the city at midnight one can hear the crash-bang of stuff being thrown out of upper-story windows: old tables or chairs, even bookcases, wine flasks, rusty pots, and the like.

To wear something new on New Year's Day brings good luck for the coming year.

In Anglo-American tradition whatever one does on New Year's Day sets the expectations for the year. So it is bad luck to stumble on New Year's Day, or to break anything, or to spend money. Don't sweep on New Year's or you will sweep out all your luck for the year.

In China, people used to pay off old debts before midnight and put up colorful posters of the gods of wealth.

Midsummer Night (JUNE 23)

This is the night to dream about your true love, because dreams dreamed on Midsummer Night are very apt to come true. A little bunch of flowers under the pillow helps this happen.

Halloween (OCTOBER 31)

If you were born on Halloween, all your dreams will come true.

It was customary in the olden times to bake many little Halloween cakes to be eaten that night. This is still a happy custom in some places today, especially at teen-age Halloween parties. A dime is baked in one and whoever happens to get that one will be rich. Whoever gets the one with the ring in it will be married soon. A little piece of clean rag is sometimes baked in one of them, and whoever eats that cake will be poor. A thimble is baked in one to show who in the party will be an old maid. And whoever gets the cake with the button in it will be an old bachelor.

Halloween used to be called Nut-Crack Night because so many nuts are eaten at Halloween parties. Roasting chestnuts in the fire till they cracked open used to be an old Halloween party pastime. Boys and girls used to name them for their boy friends or girl friends, and the nut that popped first would surely be the first one to "pop the question."

Christmas (DECEMBER 25)

It is good luck to be born on Christmas. One old English rime says:

> A child that's born on Christmas day
> Is fair and wise and good and gay.

And of course anybody like that is bound to be lucky.

It is good luck for the child who gets up first on Christmas morning and opens the door to "let Christmas in."

If you let your bayberry Christmas candles burn down to the very end, you will have good luck in the house till next Christmas.

It is very lucky to have a fly buzzing in the house on Christmas, and it is very bad luck to kill the Christmas fly.

Christmas would not seem like Christmas without the holly and mistletoe decorations through the house. And any girl caught under the mistletoe can be kissed. Christmas mistletoe must be taken down by the Twelfth Day of Christmas (January 6), however, or the boys and girls who kissed under it will never marry. But in Louisiana they say it is good luck to pick off holly berries from the Christmas decorations, because they bring luck till next Christmas.

In England the Christmas pudding was one of the features of the day. In the old days every person in the house used to have a hand in it. Every member of the family, every servant, and every guest in the house used to go into the kitchen, take a turn stirring the Christmas pudding, and make a wish. When the pudding was served, it was found to contain a ring (whoever got that would get married), a button (token that whoever got it would be an old bachelor), a little china pig (to point out the greedy one in the group), a thimble (to mark the old maid), and a shilling (to indicate who would be rich).

FOOL'S LUCK

1. Any child allowed to sleep in the moonlight will grow up to be a fool. But among all Gaelic peoples and all the peoples of India, this gift of the moon (to be a fool) means that he has special knowledge of an unseen world, no fear of supernatural things, and a special insight into the human heart. The Irish call it being *fey*.

2. If a baby never falls out of bed, it will be a fool. Many people seem to believe that a baby has to fall out of bed at least once, for luck.

3. If your nose itches, you will be kissed by a fool. Is this lucky for you, or for the fool?

4. *Fool's luck* or *a fool for luck* are old, old sayings. *Is usually luck on a fool* is the way the Irish say it. Almost everywhere people seem to think that fools are always lucky. No matter how foolish some poor fool may be, he seems always to escape the consequences of his witlessness and to emerge from every mishap with honor and success.

   People love to stick pins in balloons and hear them pop; and they love to hear fools blurt out the truth *and* expose stuffiness or pretense. The Irish especially have a great tenderness for fools, mixed with a kind of reverence. There is a mystery in them, they say, because they are in touch with some wonderful, unseen world. And there are many folktales from many parts of the world featuring the amazing good luck of some fool.

Stories about Jean Sot and Doctor Know-All, who is often named Doctor Crab, or Cricket, or Rat, are among the most famous of these. "Poor Old Cricket," the story included in this book, is a simple version of the Doctor Know-All tale as it is told in Louisiana.

JEAN SOT

"Guard the door, now," his mother said to Jean Sot one day, as she left the house to go to town. Jean said he would. She was gone so long, however, that Jean thought he had better go look for her. But he did not forget about guarding the door. He just took it off the hinges and carried it with him.

As he was going along, with the door on his back, he saw seven big rough men approaching, carrying with them a heavy sack. Jean thought the sack was surely full of money and that the men must be robbers. He was very frightened, and he thought he had better hide in a tree until they passed by.

So Jean started to climb. It was a hard job to climb a tree with a house door on his back, but he finally made it. Just in time, too.

But instead of passing by, the seven robbers stopped under that very tree and sat down in a circle and began to count out and divide the money.

"This for me—this for you—this for you—" the chief of the robbers was counting, as he made a little pile of money in front of each man.

"This for me—this for you—this for you—" he counted.

"And one for *me!*" cried Jean Sot.

"Who's that?" The men listened and heard nothing but the leaves rustling.

"This for me—this for you—this for you—" the chief began counting again.

"And one for *me!*" cried Jean Sot.

"Who's that?" cried the chief. "I'll wring the fool's neck!"

This frightened Jean Sot so much that he began to tremble, and he trembled so hard that the door slipped off his back and fell down on the robbers. The seven robbers jumped to their feet and ran off. They thought it must be the Devil himself after them if he could throw doors around like that.

Then Jean Sot climbed down from the tree and picked up all the money and went home with it.

"Not so foolish, after all," said his mother.

Jean Sot is the beloved world-wide numskull in Louisiana Cajun and Louisiana Creole guise. The name means Foolish John. Sometimes it is spelled Jean Sotte. He is the foolish boy who takes all directions literally and in spite of (or because of) his incredible stupidity comes out on top in the end.

POOR OLD CRICKET!

Once there was an old man named Cricket who knew nothing and did nothing. An old fool, people said. He was very poor and seldom had enough to eat. He was always hungry.

So he got hold of a wig somewhere, and a pair of spectacles, and a big book, and set himself up as a doctor. "I know everything," he advertised.

Just about this time a nearby king, who was very rich, discovered one day that his daughter was weeping. What was the matter? She had lost her big diamond and could not find it anywhere. Everybody looked for it but nobody could find it.

Old Doctor Cricket came along and said he could find it. The king promised him anything he desired if he could do so, but the hungry man asked only for three good big meals.

At once the king's servants laid out a sumptuous breakfast. He ate it all up and said, "Well, there's one."

The servant who was carrying out the empty dishes was terrified and nearly dropped them. The truth of the matter was that the servants had stolen the diamond, and this fellow thought the old man had found out.

After a fine lunch, which the old man ate up to the last crumb, he said, "Well, there's two." And the servants who heard the remark were more terrified than ever. Later, when he had devoured a bounteous dinner, the old doctor said, "That makes three."

The servants were now sure he was counting the ones who had stolen the diamond. They came to him secretly and promised to give it back if only he would not tell.

"All right," said the old man. "Bring it here."

When they brought it, he wrapped the big diamond up in a piece of bread and threw it to a turkey in the king's garden. The turkey gobbled up the bread, and the old man ran to the king and said, "Come see the turkey who swallowed the diamond."

So they killed the turkey and found the diamond and proclaimed the old man to be the wisest man in the world.

There were a few young men in the crowd, however, who had their doubts. They wanted to show him up for a fake. So they caught a cricket in the garden and closed it up in a box. Then they went to the old man and said politely, since he knew so much, to please tell them what was in the box.

Of course the old man did not know. How could he? He thought he was caught for a fool at last.

"Poor old Cricket!" he cried, sorry for himself.

Nobody there knew the old man's name was Cricket. They thought he just knew what was in the box. So they piled on the praise and the gifts. Lucky fool.

THE LUCKY MAN

1.

Once there was a man lying in bed asleep. And he woke up. He heard something flapping.

He got up. He walked softly to the window.

And he saw it.

It was white—flapping in the moonlight. It was under a tree. It would flap its arms out in the moonlight and then slip back into the shadow of the tree.

"It's a ghost," thought the man. "I'll fix him before he gets into the house."

Very stealthily he took his gun down off the wall where he hung it at night. And he shot holes in the flapping thing, one after another. But it went on flapping.

At last the man went back to bed. If he hadn't killed it, at least he had scared it, he thought, for it stayed in the shadow of the tree and came no nearer.

In the morning the man got up and went downstairs. His wife was already in the kitchen.

"You fool!" she said. "Shooting your clean

nightshirt full of holes!" (She had washed it the day before and hung it in the tree to dry.)

"My nightshirt!" said the man. "Gosh! Lucky I wasn't in it!"

2.

Once there was a man on horseback traveling through the world. One night he found no little inn or lighted house to give him a bed. So he lay down to sleep under a tree and tied his horse to a tree nearby.

When he woke up in the morning and opened his eyes, the horse was gone. Somebody had come along and stolen the horse in the night.

He was heavy-hearted over losing the horse and distressed because he would now have to finish the journey on foot.

Then suddenly he thought he was a lucky man.

"Lucky I wasn't sitting on the horse when it was stolen!" he said.

One day another fellow (or maybe the same one, who knows?) was walking home along a country road. He had been to town and had bought himself a new pair of boots. He was carrying them home together by the laces, across his shoulder.

It was a long, rough road, and the poor fellow was trudging along in his bare feet. Suddenly he stumbled and struck his foot against a stone. The pain was terrible.

"Lucky me!" he cried, bouncing on one foot and holding the other. "Lucky me! Lucky I didn't have the boots on!"

MONEY LUCK

1. A penny or a nickel with your birth year on it is *your* lucky coin. If you get one, always carry it with you and never part with it.

Do you wear penny-loafers? Penny-loafers are loafers with a strap to put your lucky penny in.

2. If you find a piece of money, put it in your shoe or in the middle of your loafer strap where it can't slip out—for good luck. If you never spend it, it will lead you to more.

3. If the palm of your hand itches, you are soon to get money. But let it itch. If you scratch it, you won't get any money.

4. Some people say, if your right hand itches, you will get money; if your left hand itches you will spend money.

Others say if your left hand itches, it is a sign you will receive money. Spit in your hand to make sure you will keep it.

5. If your right hand itches, put it in your pocket and very likely you will *feel* money.

6. It is good luck to dream of silver money.

7. A silver coin tied around your ankle or hung around your neck brings good luck.

8. In the British Isles, and especially in Wales, they say that to find the first daffodil of spring brings you gold.

9. When you see a falling star, if you can say "Money, money, money" before it vanishes, you will find money in your hand.

10. When you see a new moon, turn the silver money over in your pocket. This is said to make more money grow (as the moon grows).

This Anglo-Irish-American money charm is probably the ancestor of several others: show silver to the new moon—to get more money; look at the new moon with money in your hand—to bring more.

11. Spit on new money for luck before you put it in your pocket.

12. Bubbles on top of your coffee (or tea or cocoa) mean money. If you can drink them from the cup (or catch them in the spoon) before they break, the money is yours.

13.　　To dream of bees making honey
　　　Means you'll get a lot of money.

MAKING YOUR OWN

Once there was a farmer who had three strong young sons. And when the old man lay dying, he called the sons to him and said, "My whole fortune lies in one square foot of ground on this farm."

So the three sons began to dig. Sometimes they dug together, side by side, each one turning over one square foot of soil with every thrust. Sometimes they got tired and took turns. But in the end, every square foot of that farm had been dug up and turned over.

They did not find a thing. There was no box of money, no chest of gold, no sack of jewels—not a thing buried anywhere on the farm. But that year the ground, thus thoroughly worked, yielded more bounteous crops than ever before.

Then they understood what their father had meant: that their fortune was *in the farm*. And the three young sons became three rich men.

LUCKIER AND LUCKIER

This story is usually classified as a foolish bargain story. But here it is entitled "Luckier and Luckier" because Gammer Grethel, the old "story-wife of Niederwehren" (near Kassel in Germany) who told it to Jacob and Milhelm Grimm, began with the words, "Some men are born to good luck; all they do or try to do comes right."

Once there was a young fellow named Hans who worked hard for a rich farmer for seven years and got paid off with a lump of silver as big as his head.

Hans tied the lump in his kerchief, hung it over the end of his stick, put the stick across his shoulder, and started off for home to see his mother.

The lump was heavy and made his shoulder ache, but Hans tried to comfort himself by thinking of all it might buy.

After a while he saw a man coming along on horseback. When the rider stopped beside him for a few friendly words, Hans remarked how lucky a man was to have a horse, to ride along so easily and not be weighed down with a lump of silver.

"Well," the man said, "I will trade the horse for the silver and you will be rid of your load."

Hans was delighted. He gave the man the lump of silver and rode off on his horse, singing,

> No care and no sorrow
> A fig for tomorrow.

But Hans was not a skillful horseman and soon found himself hurled head over heels into the bushes.

A man coming along with a cow just then stopped the horse and helped Hans to his feet.

Hans said how peaceful it must be to walk quietly beside a cow. The man was quick to offer the cow for the horse. In a minute the trade was made and each went his way much happier than he was before.

"How lucky I am," said Hans to himself. "Now I shall always have milk and butter and cheese." And he walked along content.

Later the sun grew hot and Hans tried to milk the cow to get a drink. But the poor beast was old and dry. She had no milk. After a few minutes of Hans's clumsy efforts to milk her, she could stand it no longer and gave him a kick in the head.

Hans lay in the ditch. He was sorely disappointed in the cow. Soon along came a man with a pig in a wheelbarrow and helped him get up.

"Oh, dear!" said Hans. "My cow is no good. If it was a pig, now . . ."

"Well, I'm a butcher, myself," said the man, "and I won't say no."

So they traded. The man went off with the cow and Hans went his way leading the pig by a string. He was delighted with the world again. What luck to own a fat pig!

After a while Hans met a man carrying a goose. They stopped to chat, and Hans happily told the man about his series of bargains. Hans politely admired the goose, and it turned out that the man would be glad to trade his goose for the pig.

In a few minutes it was done. Hans walked on with the big white goose under his arm and visions of soft feather pillows in his head.

In the next village he came upon a scissors-grinder singing at his work. Hans watched the grindstone turn and the sparks fly. The man sang,

> Work light and live well
> All the world is my home.

"You are a happy man," said Hans.

"Yes," said the grinder. "There is plenty of work and plenty of money in my pocket—That's a fine goose," he added.

"Yes," said Hans and told the man his story: horse for cow, cow for pig, pig for goose.

"And what did you give for the horse?"

"A lump of silver as big as my head."

"Where did you get a lump like that?" said the man, amazed.

"I worked seven years for it."

"I see," said the man. "Now, if you had a way of finding money in your pocket every time you put your hand into it, you would be a lucky man for sure."

"I would, for sure," said Hans. "But how could that be?"

"Be a grinder!" said the man. "I will trade you the grindstone for the goose."

"Now I am the luckiest man in the world!" cried Hans. "Here! Take the goose."

"Here's the grindstone," said Hans's new friend. "And here is another stone to go with it." He picked up a big rough stone that lay on the ground nearby. "It's good to hammer nails on," he said.

So Hans took the two stones and went his way. "I was born lucky," he said to himself.

As the day wore on and the sun climbed the sky, Hans became very hot. The road was dusty; the two stones grew heavier and heavier with every step. Hans was so tired that suddenly he could go no farther.

He stopped beside a river to rest and drink the cool water. As he leaned over to drink from the stream, his foot slipped against the stones, and they both rolled into the river and sank out of sight.

Hans thanked his lucky stars to be rid of the heavy things. Now he was free and without a care in the world.

He took to the road again with a light heart and a light step. Before dark he was in his mother's house eating supper and telling her the story.

NOTHING TO LOSE

1.

There seem to be a good many folk tales revealing a kind of human awareness that it is good luck to have nothing!

There is an old Italian story about the philosopher who was shipwrecked and lost all that he owned in the sea. Many of his fellow passengers tried to hold on to their possessions and were drowned. But this man kept afloat and finally reached shore, thanking fortune that he had lost all his wealth at sea, because now, with no cares and nothing to lose, he could do as he pleased.

* * *

Did you ever hear what the little fat worried financier said when somebody asked, "What would you do if you lost all your money?"

"I'd eat bread and molasses and swing on a gate all day long."

2.

Then, there is the nursery rime about the old woman who had nothing.

There was an old woman
And nothing she had,
And so the old woman
Was said to be mad.

She had nothing to eat,
She had nothing to wear,
She had nothing to lose,
So she'd nothing to fear. . . .

As often happens, many deep-seated human attitudes and emotions turn up in nursery rimes and children's game songs.

EVERYDAY LUCK

Everyday luck is your own personal luck. It depends on whatever you do, or feel, on your own eyes, nose, mouth, and ears, and whatever happens to you, like stumbling, or sneezing, or itching.

1. How many times did you sneeze?—on what day?

Most people say it is lucky to sneeze three times in succession. In Maryland they say it is bad luck to sneeze in bed. Sometimes they say:

> Sneeze once, a wish
> Sneeze twice, a kiss
> Three times, a disappointment.

But the Japanese say that if you sneeze once, you will be praised; if you sneeze twice, you will be cursed; and if you sneeze three times, you have caught a cold.

2.　　Sneeze on Monday, sneeze for danger,
　　Sneeze on Tuesday, kiss a stranger.
　　Sneeze on Wednesday, sneeze for a letter,
　　Sneeze on Thursday, something better.

Sneeze on Friday, sneeze for sorrow,
Sneeze on Saturday, see him tomorrow!
  or—joy tomorrow
  or—see your love tomorrow
If you sneeze on Sunday, safety seek
Or the Devil will have you (get you)
  all the week.

3. It is bad luck to sneeze with your mouth full. If you wonder why, try it and see.

4. If your nose itches, company is coming, or, if you live in Maryland, good news is coming.

In England, they used to grease a child's nose on his birthday, sometimes with butter or bacon fat, sometimes with axle grease. They said it helped him "slide through the year."

5. If somebody pinches your little finger *hard*, and if you cry, that is a sign you cannot keep a secret.

6. If your fingernails have spots on them, begin with your thumb and count each finger, saying

Friend, foe, letter, beau, a journey to go
or
Friend, foe, gift, beau, a journey to go

You have as many friends as there are spots on your thumbnail, as many enemies as there are spots on the second fingernail, as many letters (gifts) to come as on the middle fingernail, and so on.

7. When do you cut your fingernails?

Cut them on Monday, cut them for health,
Cut them on Tuesday, cut them for wealth.
Cut them on Wednesday, cut them for news,
Cut them on Thursday, a new pair of shoes.
Cut them on Friday, cut them for sorrow,
Cut them on Saturday, see your sweetheart
    tomorrow.
Cut them on Sunday, bad luck.

In New England they say:

Cut them on Sunday, cut them for evil.
And be all the week as cross as the Devil.

In Worchestershire in 1835 there was a finger-nail rime, then already old, which ended:

Better a child was never born
Than cut his hoofs (nails) on Sunday.

8. Have you got a mole or a dimple? Where?

> Mole on the neck, money by the peck
> Mole on the arm, have a rich farm.

A mole on a girl's or woman's face is usually considered a mark of beauty. (In Ireland they call it a love spot.) People even used to cut out little spots of black court plaster and stick them on their faces for evening parties. They called them beauty spots.

9.
> Dimple in the chin
> Devil within.

This of course means mischief, not badness, within.

10. Have you got an *M* in the palm of your hand? If you have, that's good luck. Some people say it stands for money, some say it stands for a happy marriage; but all say it means good luck.

If you are holding hands with someone and his (or her) hands are cold, that is the sign of a warm heart. "Cold hands, warm heart" is an old, old saying.

If the palm of your right hand itches, you will

receive money, or else you will shake hands with a stranger. If your left hand itches, you are to receive money also—or spend it.

If you are just starting to do something, some little chore or job, spit on your hands for luck. All working people in Europe and the Americas know this.

11. If your ears burn, someone is talking about you. For the right ear to tingle is a good sign: someone is saying nice things.

12. When you are getting dressed in the morning, it is good luck if you put something on backward or wrong side out—accidentally, that is. It is cheating to do so on purpose. And your good luck will hold if you wear it that way and don't change it before bedtime. If you *have* to change it, get someone else to do it for you. This is entirely different from the special magic charm of wearing your sweater backward or wrong side out in order to pass an exam.

It is especially good luck if you wear something wrong side out all day long without knowing it.

13. To be sure of good luck tomorrow, be sure to place your shoes with the toes pointing under the bed when you go to sleep.

14. The way you walk and the spots where you wear out your shoes the fastest have meanings, too.

> Wear at the toe, spend as you go
> Wear at the side, rich man's bride
> Wear at the heel, spend a good deal
> Wear out the sole, live to be old
> Wear at the ball, spend all.

15. There is a lot of luck in shoes. Old shoes or slippers are thrown after a bride and groom for luck and to ensure them many children. This is a custom that goes back to ancient Indian, Jewish, and Anglo-Saxon, and old Scandinavian lore. People used to throw shoes after sailors, too, as they put out to sea, to bring them luck.

16. Don't let a button on your coat get loose enough to drop off. To drop a button means to lose a friend.

17. Mending any garment while you are wearing it brings all kinds of bad luck. It is bad luck to even darn a sock while you have it on. People seem to believe this almost everywhere in America: North, South, East, Midwest, and West. In the British Isles they say that mending, patching, or darning something while wearing it will cause people to lie about you. In Nova Scotia you will come to some

bad end for doing this. The Pennsylvania Dutch say that whoever sews or mends anything while wearing it is sewing trouble right into the seam. In Wyoming they say:

Mend clothes upon your back
Live to lack.

18. If a girl drops her handkerchief, people used to say, it is a signal to the boys that she is ready and willing to marry. The old English kissing game Drop the Handkerchief is a little drama symbolizing this custom. Another old name for this circle singing game is Kiss-in-the-Ring, because the girl who drops the handkerchief is chased and gets kissed when caught.

THE LUCKY SHIRT

Once there was a tired little king in some small kingdom long ago. He was tired because the affairs of the kingdom were not going very well. One bit of bad luck seemed to follow another, and the poor king thought no other king in the world had ever been so unlucky.

He called together his wise old men, who consulted together for three days.

"The king will be lucky when he finds a lucky man and puts on that man's shirt," they said.

So a great search was made. The king's messengers went up and down the world looking for a lucky man and to borrow his shirt.

But every man they asked had just had a bit of bad luck of one kind of another: poor crops, or money stolen, or a fine cow sickening, or a child lost—or something.

Finally they did find one old fellow who admitted he was lucky.

But—he didn't own a shirt.

MAKE A WISH

The most important thing about making a wish is never to tell it. No wish comes true, they say, if you tell. Wishes made on the new moon, on the first star, on a birthday cake, on a white horse, or on a wishbone most especially must not be told. In fact there is strong belief that just to say any wish out loud is very bad luck.

1. The Nez Percé Indians, who formerly inhabited Idaho, Washington, and Oregon, had a story about Coyote, their trickster, who was carried on the backs of five geese across a river. But when the geese came over the middle of the river, they said, "Let's drop him," so they dropped him.

When Coyote saw he was about to fall into the river, he wished himself into a feather and was soon floating lightly up and up and up. Then he was afraid of going up too high, so he said out loud, "Oh, to be an arrow!" And down he plunked —right into the river.

2. Make a wish on the first star you see at night. Say:

Starlight, star bright,
First star I've seen tonight,
I wish I may, I wish I might
Have the wish I wish tonight.

Then if you never tell the wish, it will probably come true.

In North Carolina the last line of this wishing rime sometimes goes: *See (or dream) of my true love tonight.* In the Ozarks a child usually crosses his fingers while saying the rime. A grownup spits and makes a wish. A group of college girls at Vassar in 1923 knew this rime and often said it, but added that you must not look at the star again after saying the rime if you wanted the wish to come true.

3. Light a match and make a wish. If the match burns without breaking as long as you can hold it, the wish will come true.

4. If a loose eyelash falls on your cheek, put it on the back of your hand. Shut your eyes and make a wish; then, with your eyes still shut, try to blow it off. If it is gone when you open your eyes, your wish will come true.

5. Some southern blacks say when you see a white horse, cross your thumbs and make a wish.

This was a widespread practice in the days of many horses, a relic from England. Especially wish on the first (or only) white horse you see on New Year's Day.

6. If you sleep in a strange bed, make a wish. It will probably come true. Make a wish when you sleep under a new quilt or blanket and it will come true. In North Carolina they say to make the wish while you are pulling up the new cover.

7. There is all kinds of advice about making a wish on the first sight or sound of the first creatures of spring. Country people everywhere in Europe and the British Isles, the United States, and Canada say things like:

Make a wish on the first butterfly you see in the spring.

Make a wish on the first peepers you hear in the spring.

Make a wish on the first cuckoo you hear in the spring (England, Italy, or wherever the cuckoo appears).

If you can make a wish on a redbird before it flies out of sight, the wish will come true.

Make a wish on the first robin you see or hear in the spring (New England and the Middle West).

Wish on the first toad that hops in your path in the spring.

In Alabama, children say if you can make a wish while a buzzard is flapping his wings, it will come true. This is very hard to do because the buzzard sails and glides more than he flaps.

8. You can wish on the new moon, too. Make a secret wish on the new moon and it will come true. In Louisiana they say your wish will surely come true if you make it while seeing the new moon over your left shoulder. Some people say it is luckier to wish on the new moon over your right shoulder. Take your choice about this. But all agree that it is no use to wish on the new moon through a window. You have to be outdoors.

In Tennessee they make a very special wish on the new moon. Looking at it over the right shoulder, say:

> New moon, true moon,
> True and bright,
> If I have a lover
> Let me dream of him tonight.

In North Carolina and Indiana they make this same wish on the new moon, but the rimes are slightly different.

9. Then there is the old-time custom of wishing on the wishbone of a chicken, duck, or goose. *Lucky-*

bone or *pully-bone* some people call it. When two
people pull on the wishbone, each one makes a
wish, and the one who gets the longest piece will
have his wish come true.

10. When two people happen to say the same thing at the same time, they should lock their little fingers together and each make a silent wish. They must not speak then until they say together, "Needles," and then, as they press their thumbs together, "Pins." Both wishes will come true if neither one ever tells his wish. In South Carolina they do not have to say anything. They merely lock little fingers, make a wish without speaking, and then touch thumbs.

The wonderful thing to remember about wishing is that if you wish for something long enough and hard enough, you are almost sure to get it. So you have to be very careful what you wish for.

Remember poor old King Midas who wished everything he touched would turn to gold. He nearly starved to death, for of course his meat and bread turned to gold the minute he touched them; the chicken leg in his fist was gold as soon as he picked it up; even his cup *and the water in it* turned to gold. Worst of all, when he kissed his little daughter, the pink-cheeked, laughing little girl was suddenly nothing but a gold statue. (He had a hard time getting out of that fix—but he finally did.)

SO

BE CAREFUL WHAT YOU WISH FOR
BECAUSE YOU MIGHT GET IT

BE CAREFUL!

Not long ago a certain Penobscot Indian hunter was camping near a lake with his wife and child. One night the rains came and the wind blew and a lake spirit was washed ashore by the storm.

The man found it the next morning, bedraggled and exhausted and almost dead, and he took it into the wigwam to revive it. As soon as it gained strength, he put it back into the lake. The water spirit was so grateful for this kindness that it granted the man three wishes. "Wish for anything you want," it said.

So the man went back to the wigwam and told his wife, and it was decided that each one should have a wish: first the wife, then the man, then the child.

The next day the man and his wife packed up and went to the trading post to see what they should wish for.

"You first," said the man to his wife. And while she was looking over the wares, she saw a fine broom.

"Oh! I'd like a good broom," she said, without stopping to think. And at once the broom was hers and in her hand. She had not really meant to wish for a broom, but there it was. She showed it to her husband.

He was furious. "Why did you wish for that thing," he yelled. "I wish it was your head!"

Instantly the broom was on the woman for a head. The whole long handle was down her neck with the straw part sticking up for a head. She did not like it a bit. But the poor woman could do nothing about it.

Of course there was nothing to do now but for the child to use his wish to get it off. And he did.

That's all.

THIRTEEN

Thirteen is an unlucky number. Thirteen is a lucky number. Take your choice.

The belief that 13 brings bad luck is very widespread. In Europe and America the dread is still strong and people still act upon it. Thirteen people in a group, in a room, at a table, the thirteenth day, the thirteenth *anything* is avoided because people fear that it brings bad luck and death.

It is said that in France no house is numbered 13; there is no room 13 in French hotels, no floor 13. This is true also in a number of American cities. It is true of New York hotels, apartment houses, and office buildings to some extent.

Almost everywhere people believe that it is bad luck to start a journey on the thirteenth of the month—especially on a Friday the thirteenth. In fact, on Friday, November 13, 1931, the SS *Aquitania*, scheduled to sail at midnight, did not leave her dock in New York until well after the midnight hour because of frantic requests and protests from the passengers.

1. Never set a hen on thirteen eggs. If you do, only one will hatch. This is a Georgia country saying, both black and white.

2. If a clock strikes thirteen times, that is bad luck. In Louisiana it is taken as a sign of death. Some people say it is a sign something is wrong with the clock. But in Georgia if you don't stop the clock while someone is dying, it will strike thirteen times, and then someone else in the house will die.

3. It is unlucky for thirteen people to sit at a table together; if they do, one of the group will die within a year. All thirteen may join hands and rise as one, to ward off this misfortune, but there still seems to be more fear of having thirteen at table than faith in the ceremony to ward off the bad luck. It is even bad luck (in Iowa) to have thirteen plates on the table.

In Louisiana, if thirteen dine together, either the oldest, or youngest, or the last one seated, or whoever calls attention to the fact that thirteen are present, will die.

An article in the English *Gentleman's Magazine* for 1798, discussing this fear of thirteen at table, states that certain insurance companies calculated that out of any thirteen people in a group, one would probably die within a year anyway.

There is an old Dutch proverb which says: *the thirteenth man brings death.* Some have tried to explain this association of 13 with the idea of death by pointing out that formerly in England the hangman was called "old Thirteen," because his fee was thirteen shillings. But the belief is older than that.

Some base the superstition on the fact that Jesus and His Twelve Disciples made thirteen at table at the Last Supper. Judas, the last disciple to join the group, was the thirteenth man and brought death. But the belief in 13 as a bad-luck bringer is older than that.

Perhaps the belief springs from the ancient Icelandic myth about Loki, the mischief-maker, who (uninvited) crashed the party of twelve gods who were amusing themselves casting darts at the invulnerable Balder. But Loki, the thirteenth man, brought death to Balder. The belief, however, is probably even older than that.

4. The Hill Saora people of Orissa, India, never count above twelve, because to count thirteen means death.

One day a man with thirteen sons came to a clearing in the jungle to work. A certain tiger whose brother the man had killed was hiding nearby and watching.

The man lined up his thirteen sons to count them, to see if all were there. And the minute he said "twelve," the tiger leaped out and took the thirteenth.

Now the Hill Saoras never count above twelve.

Another tale describes a group of Hill Saoras

measuring grain in a field. They measured twelve measures and, just as they were measuring the thirteenth, a tiger jumped out and killed them. Now the Saoras are afraid to count over twelve.

Dr. Elwin, who collected these myths, believes that they may have been in the oral tradition of the Hill Saora people long before Hinduism reached them. If so, they may represent the oldest of all explanations for belief in 13 as a death dealer and bringer of bad luck.

BUT

5. Thirteen is a lucky, magic number, too.

6. Any child born on the thirteenth of the month will be lucky in anything he sets out to do on the thirteenth of *any* month. In fact thirteen is his lucky number.

7. Then there is the baker's dozen: thirteen instead of twelve—thirteen loaves of bread, thirteen rolls, cakes, biscuits, tarts, or whatever comes by the dozen. That is surely a lucky thirteen! The baker's dozen goes back to the time when breads and cakes were sold by the pound in England and strict fines were imposed on bakers if they gave short weight. Thus bakers used to throw in an extra loaf or cake or tart to avoid giving short measure.

8. Jewish people feel that thirteen is a lucky number because it stands for the thirteen attributes of God. An old Jewish folksong, a number song, *Echod Mi Yodea (Who Knows One?)*, chanted toward the end of the Passover feast, declares that "thirteen are the attributes of God."

It begins with the question:

Who knows One?
I know One.
One is our God . . .

And it continues, number by number, for thirteen stanzas. The thirteenth begins:

Who knows Thirteen?
I know Thirteen.
Thirteen [are the] attributes of God.

9. And thirteen is certainly a lucky number for the United States. First came the thirteen colonies, and today we have the thirteen stripes in the flag which symbolize them. The American silver dollar shows thirteen stars, also symbolizing the thirteen colonies from which we grew, and thirteen tail feathers on the eagle. The Great Seal of the United States shows the eagle with a shield across his breast bearing thirteen red and white stripes. In

his right talon he holds an olive branch with thirteen leaves and thirteen olives; in his left he holds thirteen arrows. Over his head is a constellation of the thirteen stars.

10. American boys in the Air Force in World War II used to carry in their pockets, as a protective and good-luck talisman, an American silver dollar bearing a date which added up to thirteen: 1921 or 1912, for instance. This, along with the thirteen stars and the eagle's thirteen tail feathers, made three lucky thirteens.

There used to be thirteen buttons on sailors' pants in the United States Navy, but today they have zippers.

AUTHOR'S NOTES
AND
BIBLIOGRAPHY

The abbreviations used in this section and Bibliography are:

DFML	*Standard Dictionary of Folklore, Mythology, and Legend*
DSM	*Dictionary of Superstitions and Mythology*
ERE	*Encyclopedia of Religion and Ethics*
FBSN	*Folk Beliefs of the Southern Negro*
FCBCNCF	*Frank C. Brown Collection of North Carolina Folklore*
HIF	*Handbook of Irish Folklore*
JAF	*Journal of American Folklore*
LLS	*Lore and Language of Schoolchildren*
MAFS	*Memoirs of the American Folklore Society*
NYFQ	*New York Folklore Quarterly*
ODNR	*Oxford Dictionary of Nursery Rhymes*
SFQ	*Southern Folklore Quarterly*
WF	*Western Folklore*

The numbers in parentheses are the motif numbers as given in Stith Thompson's *Motif-Index of Folk Literature*.

Changing Luck. (1) This brief story is referred to in Clouston: *The Book of Noodles,* p. 203, citing it as part of T. F. Crane's story, "The Peasant of Larcára," in *Italian Popular Tales* (Boston, 1889), pp. 275–282. The episode belongs in the same cycle of European tales as the quest for three sillies sillier than the sillies at home.

(2) This story follows in part "Clever Elsie" (Grimm #34), in which the girl is sent to the cellar to get wine for the guest, sees the ax over her head, and weeps because someday, if she marries that young fellow and has a child, the ax might fall and kill the child.

There are many variants all over Europe and America. Sometimes it is an ax in the rafters, sometimes a heavy mallet, or a scythe, or a sword, or a butcher knife.

The tale is current also in the Punjab in India, and Stith Thompson (see *Folktale*, p. 193) believes that it comes from an original Oriental source.

Leonard Roberts, in *South from Hell-fer-Sartin*, pp. 131–133, gives a Kentucky mountain version of this famous tale. In Europe the tale falls into two types: sometimes it features the silly girl and her parents bewailing the calamity which might overtake the unborn child (J2063), and sometimes it features the quest for three persons sillier than these three, or than the man's wife (H1312.1). Usually the young fellow does come back and marry the silly but tenderhearted girl. Vance Randolph gives an Arkansas version of this tale entitled, "There's Bigger Fools Than Tildy," *JAF* 65: 162 # 5 (1955).

School Luck. **1.** Informant: Connie Coffin, Barrington, Nova Scotia—age fifteen. **2.** Connie Coffin, Barrington, Nova Scotia. **3.** Susan Murphy, Schenectady, New York. **4.** Bryant: Folklore from Edgefield County, South Carolina, *SFQ* 13:147. **5.** Opie: *LLS*, p. 214. **6.** That you will remember what you have studied if you sleep with the book under your pillow is a very general and widespread belief and is cited here from no one source. The Pennsylvania Dutch item is from A. M. Aurand, Jr.: *Popular Home Remedies and Superstitions of the Pennsylvania Germans*, p. 16. **7.** Theresa C. Brakeley, Plainfield, New Jersey. **8.** Opie: *LLS*, p. 227. **9.** General. **10.** Theresa C. Brakeley, Plainfield, New Jersey. **11.** Connie Coffin, Barrington, Nova Scotia. **12.** Susan Murphy,

Schenectady, New York. 13. *FCBCNCF* 6:418. 14. Hillary Smith, Albion, New York.

Just His Luck. This is one of the famous fables of Aesop: #157 in the Penguin edition, p. 161; #316 in the Karl von Halm collection (Teubner series, 1889). Had he fallen into the well, he would have blamed Fortune is motif N111.4.1; Fortuna tells boy to keep away from well. "I will be blamed if you fall" is motif N111.4.2 in Rotunda's *Motif-Index of the Italian Novella in Prose.*

Street Luck. 1. Bryant: Folklore from Edgefield County, South Carolina, *SFQ* 13:142. 2. Remembered from the author's childhood in New York City, c. 1900. 3. John W. Dowling, Princeton, New Jersey—who grew up in Nebraska. 4. Hendricks: Superstitions Collected in Denton, Texas, *WF* 15:9. 5. Opie: *LLS,* p. 220. 6. Ancient, traditional, and almost ubiquitous. 7. *FCBCNCF* 6:436–437. 8. The pin rimes are centuries old and traditional in the British Isles, the United States, and Canada. They were already ancient and traditional when J. O. Halliwell reported them in his *Nursery Rhymes of England,* 1842, p. 98. 9. Leach: *The Soup Stone,* p. 89. 10. From the Maritimes to Texas and westward to the Pacific in both the United States and Canada, it is good luck to see a white horse and the occasion is usually accompanied by some kind of chanted formula or specific act to make the good luck a sure thing. The same is true for the British Isles and many parts of Europe, and also for any little corner of the world where Europeans settle and have horses. 11. Hendricks: *WF* 15:9. 12. H. Roberts: Louisiana Superstitions, *JAF* 40:197. 13. Remembered from the author's childhood in Nova Scotia and New York. See also *DFML,* p. 486b. 14. Theresa C. Brakeley: remembered from childhood in Plainfield, New Jersey. 15. O'Suilleabhain: *HIF,* p. 379. 16. Maria Venturi, Rome, Italy (per Theresa C. Brakeley). See also *DFML,* p. 373c. 17. Maria Venturi, Rome,

Italy (per Theresa C. Brakeley). **18.** Remembered from the author's teen-age years. **19.** Belief in the luck inherent in found money and the efficacy of wearing it in one's shoe is widespread in Europe and America. Wearing it in one's loafer strap has been reported to me by Theresa C. Brakeley, who remembers doing so during her Plainfield, New Jersey, school days, and by Margaret C. Doane of Halifax, Nova Scotia, who was still a schoolgirl in 1961. **20.** Bryan: Children's Customs in San Mateo, *WF* 8:261.

The Lucky Beggar. This is a general European folktale, also included in Dov Neuman's *Motif-Index to Talmudic-Midrashic Literature* (Indiana University Ph.D. Thesis, 1954). Beggar escapes from fire is motif N177.

Love Luck. **1.** This saying is too common and widespread to cite any one source for it. I heard it first in my teenage years from my South Carolina mother. It is prevalent in Nova Scotia and Maine, in New York, New Jersey, Pennsylvania, Indiana, and Illinois. I have heard it also on the lips of English and German friends. In Pennsylvania they even say that just craving cucumbers means you are in love. **2.** Author's personal archives. See also *DFML*, p. 185c; Opie: *LLS*, pp. 336–337. **3.** From a little girl fourteen years old in Shelburne, Nova Scotia; also told by Bessie Smith, age eighteen, Port Latour, Nova Scotia. **4.** *FCBCNCF* 6:563. Dr. Wayland Hand reports this belief from North Carolina, Kentucky, Mississippi, Louisiana, Illinois, Iowa, Texas, Nebraska, California, New York, Ontario, and England. The author's folklore archives contain instances from New York, Indiana, and Nova Scotia. **5.** Leach: *The Soup Stone*, p. 95. **6.** *FCBCNCF* 6:486; *DFML*, p. 1031c; H. Roberts: Louisiana Superstitions, *JAF* 40: 165; *Odyssey*, xvii, p. 282. **7.** Puckett: *FBSN*, p. 504. **8.** Stout: Folklore from Iowa, *MAFS* 29:145. **9.** *DFML*, p. 186. **10.** *Ibid.*, pp. 275c, 317b. **11.** Bergen: Animal and Plant Lore, *MAFS* 7:113. **12.** *FCBCNCF* 6:567. **13.**

This belief seems to be of German origin. See Bonnerjea: *DSM*, p. 228, citing H. Ploss: *Das Weib in der Natur und Volkerkunde* (Leipzig, 1895), vol. I, p. 443. 14. McDavid: "Linguistic Geography and the Study of Folklore," *NYFQ* 14:252. 15. Bryant: Folklore from Edgefield County, South Carolina, *SFQ* 12:286.

Bad Luck Put into the Bag. Condensed from a tale entitled "Two Kinds of Luck" in *Russian Fairy Tales* (translated by N. Guterman), pp. 501–504. This book is a selection from the famous collection of 640 Russian folktales collected by Aleksander Afanas'ev into three volumes, 1855–1864. Bad luck put into the sack is motif N112.1.

Birthday Luck. 1. This is a very common saying in the United States and Canada. See also *FCBCNCF* 6:24; Bryant: Folklore from Edgefield County, South Carolina, *SFQ* 12:283. 2. H. Roberts: Louisiana Superstitions, *JAF* 40:190. 3. Opie: *ODNR*, pp. 309–310n. 4. Stout: Folklore from Iowa, *MAFS* 29:141–142, reported by informants of English, Scottish, and Norwegian descent. 5. *FCBCNCF* 6:24, 25; Whitney and Bullock: "Folklore from Maryland," *MAFS* 18:110. 6. Widespread American practice. See *DFML*, p. 144a. 7. Informant: Marion Robertson, Shelburne, Nova Scotia, 1963. 8. Well-remembered from childhood. 9. Farr: Riddles and Superstitions from Middle Tennessee, *JAF* 48:330. 10. Stout: *MAFS* 29:143. 11. *DFML*, p. 145 ab.

Friday. The old nursery rimes about being married on Friday, or sneezing, or cutting one's nails on a Friday are too well known to come from any one source. See *ODNR*, pp. 309–310 and notes, for the birth-omen rimes for the days of the week.

I am indebted to Maria Venturi of Rome, Italy (per Theresa C. Brakeley) for the Tuscan item about not laughing on Friday.

Which? Luck or intelligence is motif N141. It occurs fre-
quently in European and Indian folktales, and the idea
is a frequent favorite of the fabulists.

Holiday Luck. NEW YEAR'S DAY: *FCBCNCF* 6:365, 441;
Puckett: *FBSN*, pp. 350–351; Hendricks: Superstitions
Collected in Denton, Texas, *WF* 15; *DFML*, pp. 181b,
791a. *DFML*, p. 391a; Theresa C. Brakeley, Rome;
Puckett: *FBSN*, p. 352; *FCBCNCF* 6:493. See article
New Year by R. D. Jameson, *DFML*, pp. 790b–791a.
   MIDSUMMER NIGHT: DFML, p. 723bd.
   HALLOWEEN: *DFML*, p. 181b; Whitney and Bullock:
Folk-Lore from Maryland, *MAFS* 18:122, 123, 124.
   CHRISTMAS: Whitney and Bullock: *MAFS* 18:129.
Opie: *ODNR*, p. 309, citing J. O. Halliwell's *Popular
Rhymes and Nursery Tales*, 1849. *ERE* iii:61a. Stout:
Folklore from Iowa, *MAFS* 29:193; Speare: *More New
Hampshire Folktales*, p. 162. Kissing under the mistle-
toe is a very old European custom and thought to be,
perhaps, a vestige of some ancient fertility rite. See
DFML, p. 732ac. H. Roberts: Louisiana Superstitions,
JAF 40:192.

Fool's Luck. 1. *FCBCNCF* 6:37, citing this belief from •
North Carolina and California. Gregory: *Visions and
Beliefs*, vol. 2, p. 195. 2. This is a very general English,
European, and American saying, cited in Puckett:
FBSN, p. 342. 3. Henderson: *Folk-Lore of the Northern
Counties of England*, pp. 84–85; Stout: Folklore from
Iowa, *MAFS* 29:156, citing an informant of Norwegian
descent. 4. O'Growney: *Simple Lessons in Irish*, vol. 3,
p. 29.

Jean Sot. Leach: *The Rainbow Book of American Folk
Tales and Legends*, pp. 235–246, and p. 309 for cita- •
tions.

Poor Old Cricket! As told here, this story follows the
Louisiana version presented in Fortier: Louisiana Folk-

Tales, *MAFS* 2:16, a very simple form of the famous Doctor Know-All tale. The most famous and most typical is the European version entitled, "Doctor Know-All," #98 in *Grimms' Fairy Tales*. The oldest known version is in the Sanskrit *Katha Sārit Sāgara* or *Ocean of Story*, vol. 6, chap. 30.

There are more than four hundred versions of Doctor Know-All in the world: in Europe, Asia, Africa, and the Americas. The tale is told in Arabia, Indochina, and Indonesia; in the Philippine Islands it occurs in both Tagalog and Pampango versions. See *Grimms' Fairy Tales*, pp. 456–458; E. C. Parsons: Folk-Lore from the Cape Verde Islands, *MAFS* 15:1:188 #62 (1923) ; J. C. Harris: *Uncle Remus and His Friends* (Boston and New York, 1892), p. 24f.; M. W. Beckwith: Jamaica Anansi Stories, *MAFS* 17:151 (1924) ; D. S. Fansler: Filipino Popular Tales, *MAFS* 12:1–10 (1921). Séan O'Súilleabhain also reports it as one of the popular oral tales of Ireland. See *HIF*, p. 584, #1641. For a French-Canadian version, see Marius Barbeau and Pierre Daviault: Contes Populaires Canadiens, *JAF* 53:141–145 (1940).

The unpremeditated punning of the old man on his own name (Poor Cricket, Poor Crab, Poor Rat, and, in various Southern black tellings, "the old coon caught at last!") is motif N688. This occurs in the Sanskrit version and in most European and New World versions of the tale. The Jamaica black version has become a Jack tale, is entitled "Jack as Fortune Teller," and lacks the punning ejaculation episode. Versions from Martinique and Dominica in the Antilles also lack the punning ejaculation. See E. C. Parsons: Folk-Lore from the Antilles, *MAFS* 26:1:355, 497 (1933).

Thompson supports the theory that the tale originated in India (see *Folktale*, pp. 144–145, 292). Clouston's study of the tale, which he calls "The Lucky Imposter," comments on variants from Norway, Italy, Sicily, Turkey, Mongolia, Persia, and the famous Sanskrit original, "The Brahman Harisarman," in the

Ocean of Story. See Clouston: *Popular Tales and Fictions,* vol. 2, pp. 413–431. Y. M. Sokolov mentions the story in his *Russian Folklore* (The Macmillan Company, N. Y., 1950), p. 443.

A. M. Espinosa's Comparative Notes on New Mexican and Mexican Spanish Folk-Tales, *JAF* 27:211–231 (1914) classifies the story " 'L Adivinador" in the Doctor Know-All cycle and reinforces the Benfey-Köhler-Cosquin assumption that India is the source of the tale.

For a Porto Rican variant, see J. A. Mason and A. M. Espinosa: Porto-Rican Folktales, *JAF* 35:21 #65 (1922) entitled "El Doctor Todolosabe." Southern black versions are reported by A. H. Fauset: Negro Tales from the South, *JAF* 40:264–265 (1927), a Mississippi black telling with the "old coon caught at last" punning ejaculation; also Fauset: Riddles and Tales Collected in Philadelphia, *JAF* 41:452 (1928), from a North Carolina black informant; Zora Neale Hurston: *Mules and Men* (Lippincott, Philadelphia, 1935), pp. 111–112, from Florida.

The Lucky Man. *(1)* This story is based on the age-old numskull tale about the Turkish noodle named Khoja Nasreddin who is said to have lived about the middle of the fourteenth century.

In the story as told in Clouston's *Book of Noodles,* p. 90, he mistook his own caftan (a long-sleeved gown worn by men of the region) for a thief, shot it full of holes, and upon discovering his mistake made the famous remark that it was lucky he wasn't in it or he would have shot himself. Fool would have shot himself is motif J2235.

The anecdote is often told of the proverbial Irishman and his famous linguistic nonsense. It was popular, too, in the 1930s as one of the Little Moron stories. From Leach: *The Thing at the Foot of the Bed and Other Scary Tales,* p. 30, and p. 116 for citations.

(2) Thankful he was not sitting on the horse (ass)

when it was stolen (J2561) is another lucky man, thankful fool anecdote about Khoja Nasreddin.

(3) Fool is glad to hurt his feet instead of his shoes is motif J2199.4.1, citing Danish references. It is also the feature of one of the popular oral tales of Ireland. See O'Súilleabhain: *HIF*, p. 641.

Money Luck. 1. Personal folklore archives, with instances from South Carolina, Georgia, and Maryland. See also H. Roberts: Louisiana Superstitions, *JAF* 40:206. 2. Informants: Alice Mary Crowell, Clark's Harbor, Nova Scotia; Margaret Doane, Halifax, Nova Scotia; Theresa C. Brakeley, Plainfield, New Jersey. See also *FCBCNCF* 6:454, with instances cited from Maine, Pennsylvania, Kentucky, Alabama, Louisiana, Illinois, Texas, California. 3. Very widespread belief in the British Isles, United States, and Canada; see also *FCBCNCF* 6:446, citing items from North Carolina, Tennessee, Pennsylvania, Illinois, California, Maryland, Georgia, Florida, Maine, Indiana, Iowa, Nebraska, Washington. The item about not scratching your hand when it itches comes from Theresa C. Brakeley of Rome as part of her Plainfield, New Jersey, childhood lore. 4. Bergen: Animal and Plant Lore. *MAFS* 7:16 (item from New Hampshire). 5. Captain Benjamin Doane, Nova Scotia, c. 1900. 6. Farr: Riddles and Superstitions from Middle Tennessee, *JAF* 48:329. 7. Puckett: *FBSN*, p. 314. 8. *DFML*, p. 274b. 9. Personal folklore archives: New York street saying, c. 1900; instances also from New Jersey and Nova Scotia. See also *DFML*, p. 1009b; Stout: Folklore from Iowa, *MAFS* 29:167. 10. O'Súilleabhain: *HIF,* pp. 118, 420. See also *FCBCNCF* 6:452–454. 11. Bergen: *MAFS* 7:16 (item from New Hampshire). 12. Informant: Mary F. Moore, Pittsburgh, Pennsylvania. Personal folklore archives: instances from New York and Pennsylvania. Puckett: *FBSN*, p. 463 (Mississippi Negro), also *FCBCNCF* 6:451, citing this belief from North Carolina, Maryland, Kentucky,

Louisiana, Prince Edward Island, New Brunswick, Ontario, New England, New York, Pennsylvania, Indiana, Illinois, Ozarks, Nebraska, California, Washington. **13.** *DFML*, p. 130d.

Making Your Own. This story is best known as one of Aesop's fables: #172, p. 176 in *Fables of Aesop,* Penguin edition; #98 in the famous Karl von Halm collection (Teubner series, 1889). Father's counsel: find treasure in a foot of ground is motif H588.7, with Lithuanian and Indian (Bombay) references.

Luckier and Luckier. This story is greatly condensed from the tale entitled, "Hans in Luck," in *Gammer Grethel,* pp. 128–136. It is the same as the famous "Hans in Luck" in *Grimms' Fairy Tales,* #83, 381–386, except for a few minor details. Joseph Campbell, in his "Folkloristic Commentary," in *Grimms' Fairy Tales,* p. 856, identifies it as a townsmen's tale of fourteenth-sixteenth-century Germany. It is included in the foolish bargain cycle as motif J2081.1: foolish bargain: horse for cow, cow for pig, etc., ending up with nothing. The tale is known especially all over northern Europe. References are also given for English, Indian, Indonesian, Zuñi Indian, and Nigerian versions.

Nothing To Lose. (1) This story is the subject matter of motif J2569: philosopher thanks fortune he lost all his wealth at sea and can now devote his life to philosophy. See Rotunda: *Motif-Index of the Italian Novella in Prose,* citing *L'Hore di Ricreatione di M. Lodovico Guicciardini,* vol. 2, 1583, p. 120b. In the Latin prose collection, *Fabulae Aesopiae,* by Phaedrus in the first century A.D., this episode is attached to the Greek lyric poet Simonides of Ceos.

(2) Opie: *ODNR,* p. 430, from J. O. Halliwell's *Nursery Rhymes of England,* 1844.

Everyday Luck. 1. Most of the sneezing beliefs mentioned here are very general and widespread in the United States and Canada, springing, as they do, from the childhood rimes of English settlers in America. See Harland and Wilkinson: *Lancashire Folk-Lore,* p. 68. No one of them can be pinned down to any one state or section only. It may be interesting, however, for the reader to see Stout: Folklore from Iowa, *MAFS* 29: 157; Whitney and Bullock: Folk-Lore from Maryland, *MAFS* 18:16, 39; Leach, *The Soup Stone,* pp. 120–121. 2. See Taylor: Sneezing: A Sign of Good Luck, *WF* 20:41–42; Whitney and Bullock: *MAFS* 18:107. For a series of minor variations in this rime, see *FCBCNCF* 6:86–88. 3. An almost ubiquitous admonition to children. 4. A very general and widely diffused saying. See also H. Roberts: Louisiana Superstitions, *JAF* 40:160; Whitney and Bullock: *MAFS* 18:39; Stout: *MAFS* 29:155, from an English informant. 5. Remembered from the author's childhood; told me by my South Carolina mother. It is also mentioned by Farr as current in Tennessee. See Farr: *JAF* 48:336. 6. Remembered from the author's childhood in New York; my New Jersey cousins preferred the latter version. See also Leach: *The Soup Stone,* p. 105. 7. Like the sneezing rimes, the fingernail rimes are also too widespread to be allocated. See Harland and Wilkinson, p. 68; *DFML,* p. 379a; Johnson: *What They Say in New England,* p. 88. The Worcestershire item is from Gomme: *Popular Superstitions,* p. 133. 8. See *DFML,* p. 152cd; O'Súilleabhain: *HIF,* p. 212. 9. H. Roberts: *JAF* 40:161. 10. Leach: personal folklore and linguistic archives; Whitney and Bullock: *MAFS* 18:155. 11. This is too universal a saying to allocate. See *DFML,* p. 333c. 12. See *FCBCNCF* 6:415–417, citing such beliefs from Maryland, North Carolina, South Carolina, Kentucky, Tennessee, Alabama, Louisiana, Prince Edward Island, Nova Scotia, Ontario, New England, Maine, Massachusetts, Indiana, Illinois, Iowa, Ohio, Oklahoma, New Mexico, Nebraska, California, Oregon, Washington. Theresa C. Brakeley reports the same beliefs from Tuscany and Rome about putting garments on backward or wrong side out. **13.** Puckett: *FBSN* p. 353. **14.** Barnes: Superstitions and Maxims from Dutchess County, New York, *JAF* 36:21; Johnson: *What They Say in New England,* p. 109. **15.** *DFML,* p. 1008b; Harland and Wilkinson: pp. 264, 268; Leach: *The Soup Stone,* p. 100. **16.** Barnes: *JAF* 36:19. **17.** See *FCBCNCF* 6:429–430; Puckett: *FBSN,* p. 405; Aurand: *Popular Home Remedies and Superstitions of the Pennsylvania Germans,* p. 17.

The Lucky Shirt. The luck-bringing shirt is motif N135.3, known especially across northern Europe: Estonia, Livonia, Denmark, northern Germany. It is close kin to a story associated with Alexander the Great, who ordered a feast for those who had never known sorrow or misfortune, and nobody came (N135.3.1).

This lucky shirt tale reflects the common folk belief that certain objects can change one's luck (N135) and specifically that some special power or condition can be acquired by donning the clothes (or some garment) of a person possessing such power or condition. Magic power from donning magician's clothes is motif D1721.0.1. Thus we find here the belief that the luck of a lucky man would surely be inherent in his shirt and could be transferred.

This belief is limited to no one country, people, or culture, or time. Among certain Pueblo Indians, for instance, who believe in the curing power of the bear, the shaman, or medicine man, pulls on big mitts made of bear paws and, thus impersonating the bear, receives, and uses the curing power of the bear. See also *DFML,* article **bear medicine,** p. 126d.

Irish folktales about fairies bestowing magic shirts or cloaks on men (F343.5.1) are unrelated to this tale of the lucky shirt. They reflect belief in the magic power of fairies, not belief in the power inherent in the shirt itself.

Make a Wish. **1.** The Nez Percé Indian story told here is one incident in a longer tale given by Herbert J. Spinden: Myths of the Nez Percé Indians, *JAF* 21:150 (1908). See also article **borrowed feathers,** *DFML,* p. 157d. Trickster carried by birds and dropped is motif K1041.

2. Wishing on the first star seen at night seems to be an old and widespread practice. It has been known to the author since early childhood and I have never met a child or a teen-ager who did not already know it. The wording of the rime differs slightly from locale to locale; but it turns up surprisingly often exactly as given here. *FCBCNCF* 6:603–604, cites wishing on the first star seen at night from Germany, Ontario, North Carolina, Tennessee, Mississippi, California. See also Beckwith: Signs and Superstitions Collected from American College Girls, *JAF* 36:13; Doering: Some Western Ontario Folk Beliefs and Practices, *JAF* 51:65; Randolph: Ozark Superstitions, *JAF* 46:16; Stout: Folklore from Iowa, *MAFS* 29:143, Whitney and Bullock: Folk-Lore from Maryland, *MAFS* 18:70. Leah R. C. Yoffie also reports the rime, with slight variation, in Three Generations of Children's Singing Games in St. Louis, *JAF* 60:34.

3. Bryant: Folklore from Edgefield County, South Carolina, *SFQ* 13:146. **4.** Told to me as a small child by my mother, who was a native of South Carolina. **5.** Puckett: *FBSN,* p. 354; *DFML,* p. 504c. **6.** Farr: Riddles and Superstitions from Middle Tennessee, *JAF* 48:335; *FCBCNCF* 6:407. **7.** Bergen: Animal and Plant Lore, *MAFS* 7:40; *FCBCNCF* 6:531; Bergen: *MAFS* 7:31, 34, 40. **8.** H. Roberts: Louisiana Superstitions, *JAF* 40:152; Stout: *MAFS* 29–167; Whitney and Bullock: *MAFS* 18:9, 28, 70; Bonnerjea: *DSM,* p. 171, citing a Tennessee item from Bergen: *MAFS* 4; *FCBCNCF* 6:602. **9.** A very widespread European and American practice. **10.** Remembered from childhood in New York and performed with cousins and playmates in New Jersey, Vermont, and Nova Scotia. See also Bryant: *SFQ* 12:291.

Be Careful! This is a Penobscot Indian story collected by Dr. Frank G. Speck in the Penobscot River valley in north-central Maine, 1909–1916. (See Speck: Penobscot Tales and Religious Beliefs, *JAF* 48:84.) This was before railroads and automobile throughways had crisscrossed the old tribal hunting grounds. The people then could still remember living in wigwams, and the oldsters still knew the old tales.

This story seems to be of European origin, a tale evidently learned from early French explorers and settlers, taken over into tribal lore, and colored with Penobscot forest environment and their own earthy humor. The only liberty I have taken in retelling the tale is to have the man wish the broom onto his wife for a head instead of into her other end for a tail. The French were very early in touch with the Algonquian peoples: the Micmac Indians in Nova Scotia, the Malecites in New Brunswick, the Penobscot and Passamaquoddy groups in Maine. A telling almost identical with the Penobscot tale was found among the Malecites in 1912. See W. H. Mechling: Maliseet Tales, *JAF* 26:257 (1913).

Any child familiar with *Grimms' Fairy Tales* will recognize the similarity between this story and the famous "Three Wishes" (Grimm #87). Three foolish wishes is motif J2071. The specific motif for this story is J2075 (the transferred wish: a husband given three wishes transfers one to his wife, who wastes it; in anger he wishes the object in her body; must use third wish to get it out).

Thirteen. That thirteen is an unlucky number is too ubiquitous and lifelong a belief to be documented. Almost everyone in Europe and the Americas has heard this since childhood. References are here given only for local variations, sayings, theories, and so forth. Thirteen as unlucky number is motif N135.1.

1. Puckett: *FBSN*, p. 323. 2. H. Roberts: Louisiana Superstitions, *JAF* 40:174; Puckett: *FBSN*, pp. 82, 444. 3. Gomme: *Popular Superstitions*, pp. 133, 203–204, cites this belief in the shires for 1796; Puckett: *FBSN*, p. 404; Henderson: *Folk-Lore of the Northern Counties of England*, p. 33; Stout: Folklore from Iowa, *MAFS* 29:160, 161; H. Roberts: *JAF* 40:194. 4. Elwin: *Tribal Myths of Orissa*, pp. 417, 418; 417n1 cites W. Fawcett: On the Saoras, *Journal of the Anthropological Society of Bombay* 1:242 (1888). 5. Thirteen as magic number is motif D1273.1.6, citing Jewish and other United States references. 6. *FCBCNCF* 6:25, citing a Kentucky item. 7. Personal folklore archives. 8. See Leah R. C. Yoffie: Songs of the Twelve Numbers and the Hebrew Chant of Echod Mi Yodea, *JAF* 62:383 (1949); Ruth Rubin: Some Aspects of Comparative Jewish Folksong, in *Studies in Biblical and Jewish Folklore*. 9. Wallrich: Superstition and the Air Force, *WF* 19:11.

BIBLIOGRAPHY

A. Monroe Aurand, Jr.: *Popular Home Remedies and Superstitions of the Pennsylvania Germans*. The Aurand Press, Harrisburg, Pennsylvania, 1941

Gertrude Barnes: Maxims and Superstitions from Dutchess County, New York, *JAF* 36:16–22 (1923)

Martha Warren Beckwith: Jamaican Folklore, *MAFS* 21 (1929)

————: Signs and Superstitions Collected from American College Girls, *JAF* 36:1–15 (1923)

Fanny Bergen: Animal and Plant Lore, *MAFS* 7 (1899)

Biren Bonnerjea: *Dictionary of Superstitions and Mythology*, Folk Press Ltd., London, 1927

Frank C. Brown Collection of North Carolina Folklore:
Popular Beliefs and Superstitions, vol. 6 (ed. Wayland
D. Hand), Duke University Press, Durham, North
Carolina, 1961

N. R. Bryan: Children's Customs in San Mateo, WF
8:261 (1949)

Margaret M. Bryant: Folklore from Edgefield County,
South Carolina, SFQ 12:279–291 (1948); 13:136–148
(1949)

W. A. Clouston: Popular Tales and Fictions, 2 vols., William Blackwood and Sons, Edinburgh and London, 1887
————: The Book of Noodles, Elliott Stock, London, 1888

J. F. and E. E. Doering: Some Western Ontario Folk Beliefs and Practices, JAF 51:60–68 (1938)

Verrier Elwin: Tribal Myths of Orissa, Oxford University
Press, London, 1954

Fables of Aesop (tr. S. A. Handford), Penguin Books,
Baltimore, 1954.

T. J. Farr: Riddles and Superstitions from Middle Tennessee, JAF 48:318–336 (1935)

Folklore in the News, WF 18:326 (1959)

Alcée Fortier: Louisiana Folk-Tales, MAFS 2:63–69
(1895)

Gammer Grethel: German Fairy Tales and Popular
Stories as Told by Gammer Grethel, translated from
the collections of MM Grimm by Edgar Taylor, H. G.
Bohn, London, 1863

Sir Laurence Gomme: Popular Superstitions, Elliott
Stock, London, 1884

Lady Augusta Gregory: Visions and Beliefs in the West
of Ireland, 2 vols., G. P. Putnam's Sons, New York and
London, 1920

Grimms' Fairy Tales (with commentary by Joseph Campbell), Pantheon Books, New York, 1944

John Harland and T. T. Wilkinson: Lancashire Folk-
Lore, Frederick Wayne and Co., London, 1867

Joel Chandler Harris: Uncle Remus, His Songs and Sayings: The Folklore of the Old Plantation, New York
and London, 1915

Henry H. Hart: *700 Chinese Proverbs*, Stanford University Press, California, 1954

James Hastings: *Encyclopedia of Religion and Ethics*, 13 vols., Charles Scribner's Sons, New York, 1908–1927

W. Henderson: *Notes on the Folk-Lore of the Northern Counties of England and the Borders*, Folk-Lore Society, London, 1879

G. D. Hendricks: Superstitions Collected in Denton, Texas, *WF* 15:9f. (1956)

Homer: *The Odyssey* (tr. E. V. Rieu), Penguin Books, Baltimore, 1951

Clifton Johnson: *What They Say in New England*, Lee and Shepard, Boston, 1896

William Jones: *Credulities Past and Present*, Chatto and Windus, London, 1898

Maria Leach: Personal archives of folklore and linguistics
————: *The Soup Stone: The Magic of Familiar Things*, Funk and Wagnalls Company, New York, 1954
————: *The Rainbow Book of American Folk Tales and Legends*, The World Publishing Company, Cleveland and New York, 1958
————: *The Thing at the Foot of the Bed*, The World Publishing Company, Cleveland and New York, 1959
————: *Noodles, Nitwits, and Numskulls*, The World Publishing Company, Cleveland and New York, 1961
————: *God Had a Dog*, Rutgers University Press, New Brunswick, New Jersey, 1961
———— and Jerome Fried: *Standard Dictionary of Folklore, Mythology, and Legend*, 2 vols., Funk and Wagnalls Company, New York, 1949–1950

Raven I. McDavid: Linguistic Geography and the Study of Folklore, *NYFQ* 14:242–258 (1958)

Rev. Eugene O'Growney: *Simple Lessons in Irish*, 20th ed., 5 vols., Gaelic League, Dublin, 1920

Iona and Peter Opie: *The Lore and Language of Schoolchildren*, Oxford University Press, Oxford, 1959
————: *Oxford Dictionary of Nursery Rhymes*, Oxford University Press, Oxford, 1951

Séan O'Súilleabhain: *Handbook of Irish Folklore*, Folklore of Ireland Society, Dublin, 1942

N. N. Puckett: *Folks Beliefs of the Southern Negro*, University of North Carolina Press, Chapel Hill, 1926

Vance Randolph: Folktales from Arkansas, *JAF* 65:159–166 (1952)

Hilda Roberts: Louisiana Superstitions, *JAF* 40:144–208 (1927)

Leonard Roberts: *South from Hell-fer-Sartin: Kentucky Mountain Tales*, Kentucky University Press, Lexington, 1955

D. P. Rotunda: *Motif-Index of the Italian Novella in Prose*, Indiana University Publications, Folklore Series, Bloomington, 1942

Ruth Rubin: Some Aspects of Comparative Jewish Folksong, *Studies in Biblical and Jewish Folklore* (ed. Raphael Patai, Francis Lee Utley, and Dov Noy), Indiana University Press, Bloomington, 1960

Russian Fairy Tales (tr. Norbert Guterman), Pantheon Books, New York, 1945

Mrs. Guy E. Speare: *More New Hampshire Folktales*, Plymouth, New Hampshire, 1936

Frank G. Speck: Penobscot Tales and Religious Beliefs, *JAF* 48:1–107 (1935)

Herbert J. Spinden: Myths of the Nez Percé Indians, *JAF* 21:150 (1908)

Samuel G. Stoney and Gertrude M. Shelby: *Black Genesis*, The Macmillan Company, New York, 1930

Earl Stout: Folklore from Iowa, *MAFS* 29 (1936)

Archer Taylor: *The Proverb*, Harvard University Press, Cambridge, 1931

———: Sneezing, A Sign of Good Luck, *WF* 20:41–42 (1961)

Stith Thompson: *The Folktale*, Dryden Press, New York, 1946

———: *Motif-Index of Folk Literature*, 2d ed., 6 vols., Indiana University Press, Bloomington, 1955–1958

Bill Wallrich: Superstition and the Air Force, *WF* 19:11–16 (1960)

A. W. Whitney and C. C. Bullock: Folk-Lore from Maryland, *MAFS* 18 (1925)

Irene Yates: A Collection of Proverbs and Proverbial Sayings from South Carolina Literature, *SFQ* 11:187–199 (1947)

Leah R. C. Yoffie: Three Generations of Children's Singing Games in St. Louis, *JAF* 60:1–51 (1947)

————: Songs of the Twelve Numbers and the Hebrew Chant of Echod Mi Yodeà, *JAF* 62:383 (1949)

MARIA LEACH is probably best known as compiler-editor of the distinguished two-volume *Standard Dictionary of Folklore, Mythology, and Legend*—the product of more than twelve years' research. American folklore has long been a special interest of hers, particularly in the areas of dialects, folk speech, and slang, and her love of the subject led to the writing of *The Rainbow Book of American Folk Tales and Legends*. She is also the author of *The Soup Stone: The Magic of Familiar Things, The Beginning: Creation Myths Around the World, The Thing at the Foot of the Bed and Other Scary Tales*, and *Noodles, Nitwits, and Numskulls*, all for children. *God Had a Dog: Folklore of the Dog* is her most recent book for adults. Mrs. Leach lives in Nova Scotia and is a member of the American Folklore Society, of which she has been a Councillor, of the American Anthropological Association, the American Dialect Society, the Canadian Folk Song Society, the Northeast Folklore Society, and the American Indian Ethno-historic Conference.